"You will not ne
yourselves, stand s

2 Chronicles 20:17

Revised Printing 2003

A Call To Duty – God's Call For Spiritual Positioning in the Body of Christ For End-Time Ministry

Published by *Spirit of Truth Publishing*
Tulsa, Oklahoma 74153

Cover design by *Ron Blanchard Productions*

Printed in the United States of America.

A Call To Duty

God's Call for Spiritual Positioning in the Body of Christ for End-Time Ministry

by
Linda Montgomery

TABLE OF CONTENTS

FOREWORD

When an author takes pen to paper and opens the reader's heart to share their passion, they're taking a major risk. For the reader, encountering the heartfelt passion of the author's words will cause their own hearts to be searched, and thus put those words to careful scrutiny.

Linda Montgomery has taken such a risk in writing this book. Her passion for God, His Word, His Church, and His work certainly broadcasts a heart-searching beacon that will look into your heart with every page you turn. As you begin to carefully examine her message, you will understand the measure by the only standard we as Christians are to live by, our Lord Jesus Christ. What she says in her writing is worthy of the most careful scrutiny. For the truth expressed in this book is truly a wake-up call to the body of Christ and must be heard loud and clear, as well as heeded by every saint.

Linda is a wonderful, vivacious, multi-talented woman of God. She is a woman of the Word who walks with God by faith, in prayer and loving ministry. Linda has learned to live in His glory, fearing Him alone, in tune with His voice and readily obedient to His every direction.

She has taken on the call of God on her own life as a lifestyle. Therefore, she is well-suited to write to the Church she loves so much, to encourage all believers to wake up, hear His call and do it.

Based on the life and ministry of Deborah, Linda illustrates her insights into this Biblical character and the history surrounding the events of Deborah's life that are at once thorough and profound. She has uncovered every nugget of truth to be found in this historic account, and the insights are profound in her uncanny ability to bring them to life with up-to-date personal application for every reader.

This book will cause you to reflect upon your own life, meditate upon God's specific call for you, and convict you to respond and take immediate action.

Steve Purdue, Sr. Pastor
Coastland Foursquare Church
Huntington Beach, CA

Dedicated to the great heroes
of faith who endured the
call.

INTRODUCTION

As the prophetic clock continues to tick more intensely in this final hour, the Church expectantly awaits another great move of God.

The major restoration movements have come and passed: The Protestant Movement (1500's), the Evangelical Movement (1600's), the Holiness Movement (1700's), the Faith Healing Movement (1800's), the Pentecostal Movement (1900's), the Latter Rain Movement (1950's), the Charismatic Movement (1960's), the Faith movement (1970's), the Prophetic Movement (1980's), and the Apostolic Restoration (1990's).

When God gets ready to do something "new," **He always makes preparation in His people, His product, and His place for ministry.** The 1990's by far have proven to be a major turning point for the Church. History has proven the careful preparation of God's people for *"such a time as this"* through these major restoration movements.

Now, more than ever, each of these movements are lining up into one powerful move of God for the greatest end-time ministry ahead! A spirit of *Evangelism* has rebirthed here in the United States; *Holiness* has become a renewed vision of the people of God. Where church history and *Protestant* reformation had been placed on a back burner, a spirit of revival is returning to the understanding and hearts of men. *Pentecostalism* has become more understood and liberated by the body of Christ, and *Charismatics* are fanning the flames of the gifts of the Spirit throughout the body of Christ. The *Latter Rain* has poured out the necessary anointing to empower all of God's people, the *Prophetic* voice of God is going forth in greater magnitude than ever, and the *Apostolic* age is upon us as both men and women rise up and become spiritual fathers and mothers they've been called to be.

Today, God is preparing His people for a new move of His Spirit—a move that will commission a *positioned* people of God. But first, He will position those He has prepared for this great end-time ministry. And, in order to fulfill His plan, God is calling His people to commune with Him in a deeper, more intimate relationship, revealing new direction and vision to position those He has called to duty.

I believe God is resounding loud and clear His word, ***"Position yourselves, stand still and see the salvation of the Lord..."*** (2 Chronicles 20:17). And, I believe with all my heart God has called you to an appointed position for an appointed time to fulfill this great move of God.

Are you hearing His voice in this finest hour? Are you prepared, positioned and ready to see the next great move of God? In the following chapters, it is my privilege to challenge you with *A Call To Duty,* a most vital message for the Church today. It is my prayer that this living Word from God will spark forth revival within the heart of every reader.

For the Harvest,

Linda Montgomery

CHAPTER ONE

WAKE-UP CALL

Awake, awake, Deborah, awake, awake, sing a song.

Judges 5:12

It's 3:30 in the morning!, I thought to myself as I focused my eyes across the bedroom to the bright green digits on my alarm clock. *Why are my eyes wide open, Lord? The alarm clock hasn't gone off yet – so, why am I lying here in the dark of early morning, wide awake?*

There seems to be something really powerful going on in the upper planning room when divine wake-up calls occur in the wee hours of the morning. The psalmist Asaph expressed his own experience such as this in Psalm 77:4-6:

You hold my eyelids open; I am so troubled that I cannot speak. I have considered the days of old, the years of ancient times. I call to remember my song in the night; I meditate within my heart, and my spirit makes diligent search.

Sometimes when we're so busy in the day, the only time God can get our undivided attention is in the silence of the early morning hours. And, so it is for some people. I remember when I formerly preferred to hear from God according to my schedule and when I was ready, rather than according to His schedule and when He was ready. But, even though our frustration of unwillingness dribbles across our sleepy mind, the timing and the purpose of God's voice is always perfect—even at 3:30 in the morning.

A SONG IN THE NIGHT

Many times we will hear from God for answers to our prayers, or confirmations to His word for us, or to receive personal conviction. But in the Church's final hour, I believe God desires to communicate to us in a deeper, more intimate relationship, revealing new direction to His people—a *"song in the night"* to position those called for end-time ministry.

Throughout the Bible, God has communicated to His people by revealing to them a prophetic song when victory had been won, such as the song of Moses (Exodus 15:1-19), the song of Miriam (Exodus 15:20-21), the song of Deborah and Barak (Judges 5:1-31), the songs of David (Book of Psalms), the song of Pentecost (Acts 2:4), the song of spiritual baptism in the believer (Acts 19:6), and the new song of the raptured Church (Revelation 5:9-10).

Today, God is revealing a song of victory to His people through His spoken Word (or *rhema*) in order to position the body of Christ into a greater dimension of the Holy Spirit for end-time ministry.

God has and always speaks to His people in three ways: Through the written word of God, through the spoken *rhema* or word of God by the prophets, and through His Holy Spirit which is through all three. Today, God desires to walk and talk with us in an individual, personal, and intimate relationship. Yet, not all Christians understand how to recognize the word of the Lord. Even with they do recognize it, many do not know how to respond to it so that it can be fulfilled.

In the beginning of the early Church, the apostle Peter was one of the first who heard God's voice for himself. When Jesus asked His disciples, ***"Who do you say that I am?"*** (Matthew 16:13-15), Peter responded to Him saying, ***"You are the Christ, the Son of the living God"*** (verse 16). Jesus then replied, ***"Blessed are you, Simon Bar-Jonah, for flesh and blood has not revealed this to you, but My Father who is in heaven"*** (verse 17).

Peter had entered into a greater dimension of divine communication with his heavenly Father, not by hearing someone else's report (the flesh), nor by witnessing the life, death, burial and resurrection of Jesus (the Blood), **but by the Holy Spirit—"for the Spirit searches all things, yes, the deep things of God"** (1 Corinthians 2:10).

And, it is vital that we do not refuse to hear God's voice when He speaks to us as the Scripture warns in Hebrews 12:25:

> **See that you do not refuse Him who speaks. For if they did not escape who refused Him who spoke on earth, much more shall we not escape if we turn away from Him who speaks from heaven...**

Our heavenly Father will speak to us today when we are willing to draw into the deep things of His Holy Spirit, receiving divine revelation and the fullness of His Spirit to maturity—**"Draw near to God and He will draw near to you"** (James 4:8). He will reveal to you a **"song in the night."**

There is a time and a season for everything, and now is the season for the body of Christ to hear from heaven and take hold of the prophetic voice of God in order to set themselves in the position to which they are specifically called. But in order to do this, it will take **discipline** and **a spiritually-tuned ear** to hear God's voice in this final hour.

TRUE GLORY

The prophetess Deborah received a wake-up call from God in order to stir up the other leaders who had neglected (and even rejected) their designated positions to which they had been called by God:

> **Then she [Deborah] sent and called for Barak the son of Abinoam from Kedesh in Naphtali, and said to him, "Has not the Lord God of Israel commanded, 'Go and deploy troops at Mount Tabor; take with you ten thousand men of the sons of Naphtali and the sons of Zebulun; and against you I will deploy Sisera, the commander of Jabin's army, with his chariots and his multitude at the River Kishon; and I will deliver him into your hand'?"**
>
> **Judges 4:6-7**

and,

> **Barak said to her, "If you will go with me, then I will go; but if you will not go with me, I will not go!" So she said, "I will surely go with you; nevertheless there will be no glory for you in the journey you are taking, for the Lord will sell Sisera into the hand of a woman." Then Deborah arose and went with Barak to Kedesh.**
>
> **Judges 4:8-9**

Hearing God's voice, Deborah prophesied to God's people the precise battle plan that God had spoken to her and the men determined by God who would be deployed for duty. Barak, on the other hand, was **deaf to the call of God,** and was not readily willing to go alone. God had called Barak to his appointed position, and even though he was "equipped" with gifts and talents for the mission, **he didn't contain the true glory of God** and was "spiritually unprepared" for duty. For Barak, his focus was elsewhere **restricting him from lining up with the supernatural strategies that God had set before him.**

Through God's grace, however, Deborah was sent to build up and encourage Barak for the duty he had been called to. Note also, that Barak would have **"no glory in the journey"** because of the lack of communication with his heavenly Father. From his book, *The Father's Discipline,* Pastor Gary McIntosh explains that this glory can only be contained by men and women of God who are fully submitted vessels to the Father's discipline:

> *"The Father is not coming this time with just talents and gifts, but with order and discipline so that we are stable and secure for the times ahead. He is coming to establish vessels of*

integrity and character. ***These will be the only vessels able to contain the glory.*** *There may be some preachers who can move you and then claim God's glory,* ***but you won't be changed unless the true glory is present.*** *Unless Almighty God invades your life and you allow Him to build you, there will only be moments of thrills and chills instead of a lifetime of intimate relationship."*[1] (Emphasis mine.)

Here, the key to God's glory is founded on the intimate relationship with our heavenly Father. Though many Christians have been blessed and have blessed others with their various spiritual gifts and talents, many have never tasted the true glory of the Lord! Oh, you might have been in His presence, but to "contain" His glory in the fullness of His presence only comes through the intimate communion with our heavenly Father by divine order and discipline.

Paul said, **"For if the ministry of condemnation** [the law] **had glory, the ministry of righteousness** [the Spirit] **exceeds much more in glory"** (2 Corinthians 3:9). To contain the glory of the Lord is a privilege. It cannot be purchased. It is the desire of the Holy Spirit to take full control of God's vessels, anytime, anywhere, and at any cost through those who desire to live holy lives for Him.

I remember attending one of the meetings of healing evangelist, Kathryn Kuhlman during my teenage years. I was not saved, and it was quite evident. I had been a runaway, on drugs and suicidal for most of the time. I was far from holy living. But my aunt insisted that my mother and I go to hear Miss Kuhlman preach.

After wrestling with the devil several hours before my aunt picked us up, there we sat at the Shrine Auditorium in Los Angeles, California in September 1971. I clearly remember seeing Miss Kuhlman stroll back and forth on the platform, her long chiffon gown flowing along behind her. I thought to myself, *This woman is no rock star, but she's pretty far out!* Her voice as she preached was not an ordinary woman's voice. It had power and authority in it.

After she finished preaching, my aunt insisted that I go down to the altar to have Miss Kuhlman pray for me. After she literally booted me down the aisle from the stadium's upper balcony level, by a miracle, I reached my way to the platform. [There must have been over 1,000 other people trying to get up onto the platform but couldn't because it was overcrowded.] Instantly, however, I found my way up onto the platform. As I stood face to face with Miss

Kuhlman, I saw what looked like fire blazing in her eyes, and as she stretched her hand toward me, my whole body went numb. The next thing I remembered was two men helping me to stand back up on my feet. Exactly seven days later, I had been totally healed of a prolonged infection in my feet that three other doctors had tried to cure, but failed. Glory to God!

You see, God can bring healing, joy and peace, just from being **in the presence of His glory.** This is what it is meant by the glory according to the **"ministry of condemnation"** [the law]. How much more, then, shall God do through His vessels who **contain** His glory! For, **"the ministry of righteousness** [the Spirit] **exceeds much more in glory"**!

FROM GLORY TO GLORY

An intimate relationship with our heavenly Father comes only through a spiritual mind-set and a spiritual walk with Jesus Christ. In this relationship with Christ, you will think like Christ, hear like Christ, see things like Christ, speak sound words like Christ, and will contain the same passion Christ had for His heavenly Father. Paul describes in 2 Corinthians 3:18:

> **But we all, with unveiled face, beholding as in a mirror the glory of the Lord, are being transformed into the same image from GLORY TO GLORY, just as by the Spirit of the Lord."** (Emphasis mine.)

When I was a young girl, I would tell everyone, "I want to be just like my daddy." In the spiritual sense, I want my character and being to be transformed into the image of my heavenly Father. When we become vessels of integrity and character in the image of our God, we will be vessels who contain the true glory of God. As we are being transformed from glory to glory, how much of His glory we contain is left up to us.

Because of Christ, we have divine access to come boldly before the heavenly throne of God. But, even though Jesus restored divine communication for all who have been bought by His Blood, the open line of communication is **NOT** open at **ALL** times! **It can be blocked by spiritual wickedness in our own lives!** Lack of prayer, fellowship, or praise and worship tears down the spiritual optical fibers that link His heavenly signals to our earthly receivers. Instead of God receiving our willing response to His voice, He instead receives our "busy" signals.

WHO WILL PREPARE FOR BATTLE?

Deborah, being spiritually in tune with God's voice, had an intimate relationship with God who appointed her to a position to coordinate a complex mission. Her intimate times were most likely spent under a palm tree (Judges 4:5) where people came up to her for judgment. When she was called by God to a special mission to defeat king Jabin and Sisera and his powerful army, she, not only being equipped for the mission but also spiritually prepared for her position, went out with great authority and understanding of God's divine strategy for that hour. She sang a song of victory—the victory song from which the divine revelation of God became the spoken Word (or rhema) to her innermost being.

As God speaks to us today through His Word, His people, and His Holy Spirit, this supernatural transformation of the *Logos* (the inspired **written** Word of God) along with the divine revelation of God's Word through the Holy Spirit, will release a *rhema* (the inspired prophetic **spoken** Word of God) into our innermost being for a new, fresh vision and direction. This ignites the prophetic Word within our spirit-man that releases the perfect will of God for our lives.

Dr. Bill Hamon, founder and president of Christian International Network of Prophetic Ministries, says:

> *"When we use the term 'Logos,' we mean the Scriptures as a whole; when we say 'rhema,' we mean a specific Word from the Lord that applies the Logos to us individually. Though the Logos never changes or fails, the Bible is full of rhemas to individuals that never came to pass. Actually, however, in these cases it was not the rhema of the Lord that failed, but rather the people who heard it failed to understand, interpret, believe, obey, respond, wait upon, or act upon it according to God's will and way. This is the meaning of 1 Corinthians 13:8: 'Prophecies shall fail.'"*[2]

The prophet Amos also describes the divine revelation of God:

> **Surely the Lord God does nothing, unless He reveals His secret to His servants the prophets. A lion has roared! Who will not fear? The Lord God has spoken! Who can but prophesy?**
>
> **Amos 3:7-8**

In addition to hearing the voice of God, we must also understand the times and the seasons in which we are called. Even as Deborah was surrounded by the princes of Issachar (Judges 5:15), **"men who had understanding of the times,"** likewise our thoughts and meditations need to be in tune with the voice of God, and surrounded by godly men and women who can prophesy to confirm God's spoken Word in our lives. These Words of prophecy will by no means predict an unfamiliar blueprint of God's direction for your life, **but will reveal and confirm what God has already spoken to you through His Word, His people and His Holy Spirit!**

There are some areas of caution to take in the prophetic ministry today just as Jesus warned, for false prophets have become accustomed to end-time ministry. **"For if the trumpet makes an UNCERTAIN SOUND, who will prepare for battle?"** (1 Corinthians 14:8). But remember, whenever you're wakened by the roaring Lion, no matter what the hour may be, get ready to receive all that God has to speak to you. Take your position and take hold of the prophetic Word he will reveal to you to reach your destiny. Be not only equipped with gifts and talents for the battle, but be prepared for duty by becoming spiritually in tune with the voice of the Lord! Then, **"who can but prophesy?"**

CHAPTER TWO

MISSION IMPOSSIBLE MADE POSSIBLE

Then the survivors came down, the people against the nobles; The Lord came down for me against the mighty."

Judges 5:13

Just when you think God has left you on the comfortable sideline of the battlefield, along comes a loud voice from heaven, revealing to you a fresh vision for the kingdom of God. *But Lord, well--that, seems "impossible" —for me! There's just not enough financial support; my wife/husband wouldn't be in agreement with this; I've got too many roots in this position for me to just walk away from it; I've never done that before and I don't think it's my calling,* and the list of never-coulds goes on and on.

Whatever vision and calling God has blessed you with, getting from plan A to plan B can sometimes appear in the natural eye to be impossible. While walking between a rock and a hard place, confusion becomes your number one enemy. We can become so discouraged even by just comparing ourselves with others in the body of Christ. Even so much that we begin to judge ourselves "doomed" instead of "bloomed" for the ministry.

BLOCK-"ADES" AND BLOCK-"AIDES"

Too many times WE are the cause for the blockades placed in the way of our divine calling. We take the assignment God has so graciously laid out before us and begin stacking block upon blocks of fear, despair, doubt, and discouragement in the pathway of our vision. Or, in some cases, there is sin that has not been dealt with and we are in need of repentance in order to remove those blocks.

Paul repeatedly warned the church at Corinth of their blockades caused by sin and various lusts by their own affections:

> **You are not restricted by us, but you are restricted by your own affections."**
>
> **2 Corinthians 6:12**

These people of God could not live victorious lives or walk in the fullness of their calling because their own affections restricted them from doing so. Only when they would put away all of their materialistic and self-satisfying desires would these blockades and restrictions be removed.

Israel struggled most of the time with sin, fear and discouragement. In the time of Deborah (Judges 4-5), Israel was a backslidden people of God who worshiped the idols of the Canaanites, and were left as slaves oppressed by king Jabin, and Sisera and his powerful army. Israel became spiritually "dead" and "deserted":

> **In the days of Shamgar, son of Anath, in the days of Jael, the highways were deserted, and the travelers walked along the byways, village life ceased, it ceased in Israel...until I Deborah arose...**
>
> **Judges 5:6-7**

In the bleak moment of Israel's despair, Deborah arose to lead God's people back to the vision He had given them. By God's grace, Israel survived the blockades placed in the pathway of their vision:

> **Then the survivors came down, the people against the nobles; the Lord came down for me against the mighty.**
>
> **Judges 5:13**

AFFLICTION-101

For every believer, God's school of grace includes a course in Affliction-101:

For You, O God, have tested us; You have refined us as silver is refined. You brought us into the net; You laid affliction on our backs. You have caused men to ride over our heads; we went through fire and through water; BUT YOU BROUGHT US OUT TO RICH FULFILLMENT (Emphasis mine.)

Psalm 66:10-12

Okay, so now you're asking, "Why would God allow men to ride over our head, when by faith we are the head and our enemies are the tail?" **(And the Lord will make you the head and not the tail,** Deuteronomy 28:13). According to Psalm 66:10-12, God is the Head and we are His handiwork—a vast difference! God is not giving the devil dominion over us. No, instead, God is acting as our Purifier and Refiner, perfecting us for a greater blessing!

God **will** cause men to ride over your head. He will bring you through the fire in order to melt down all of the useless things in your life, and He will bring you through the water to immerse you deep into the flexible capacities of God, beyond the limitations of our own understanding and knowledge. But the rewards on your report card will be worth it all, because God will bring you into a deeper place—a richer fulfillment—a greater anointing!

Note also, that only the "survivors" will be placed in their appointed positions. God is *for* those who have survived Affliction-101. No matter what round you're in, be assured that when it's all over, you're a winner! And, during each round, don't tell God how big your opponent is; instead, tell your opponent how big your God is!

When we're obedient to live for Christ in all that we say and do, God is faithful to fulfill the promises for each of us. He can remove the blockades in the pathway of our vision. **But He can also place block-"aides" in the pathway of our vision** in order to refines us for a greater work prepared ahead.

I remember one season in my life when I was praying and believing God for a breakthrough in coordinating a trip to Israel. I felt the time was right and that God's "Macedonian call" was sure. But it *wasn't.* Door after door began to close and I was rebuking what I thought was satan's hindrances. After months of getting refocused in the Word and prayer, I discovered that God was redirecting my steps toward the pathway of the vision according to His perfect will, thus causing the trip to Israel to be impossible. As I received new confirmation through His Word and others, I could only praise Him for placing those block-"aides" into my pathway. Soon thereafter, God began to open new doors of ministry elsewhere—opportunities I had never imagined before. The impossible mission became a possibility of greater opportunity for me to minister in areas in which I could not see before.

BUT THOSE WHO WAIT…

Whatever vision the Lord has placed on your heart, if it is truly God who has spoken it to you, then you will know your calling is sure. Nothing will be impossible for you to see your vision fulfilled. It might take a year, or two years; it might even take five or ten to see God bring it to pass—but **"He who promised is faithful"**:

> **For since the beginning of the world men have not heard nor perceived by the ear, nor has the eye seen any God besides You, WHO ACTS FOR THE ONE WHO WAITS FOR HIM** (Emphasis mine.)
>
> **Isaiah 64:4**

Even though we may have to wait on God for His perfect timing and His perfect will for ouor lives, He will act for those of us who wait for Him!

CHAPTER THREE

DIVISION: THE BEAST OF WAR

These six things the Lord hates...a proud look, a lying tongue, hands that shed innocent blood, a heart that devises wicked plans, feet that are swift in running to evil, a false witness who speaks lies, and one who sows discord among brethren.

Proverbs 6:16-19

From the dark crevices of wickedness in this world, there is still yet another beast who prowls day and night among the body of Christ, seeking whom he may devour. His name is "Division," the beast of war.

You can visibily see him at work in the media and the Church. He is running rampant among heresy hunters and others who desire to destroy the body of Christ. He attacks various Christian denominations with varied denominational differences, aside from basic orthodox views, and various people of color and cultural diversities who attempt to dwell in unity among the brethren. He strikes the most unimaginable places—the Church, and he uses the latest state-of-the-art technology—the media.

I know of one dear brother in Christ who has faced the firing squad of false accusation over the past two years for publishing a book written with love to bring unity and restoration among those attacked by someone in the body of Christ and the media. Even the publishers of his book were falsely accused as an attempt to discredit them for future publishing of the book.

I sat amazed as I read over every document submitted to and from these men of God and their accusers, and I was shocked by the evidence of lies told about these men of God by other certain men in the body of Christ and the secular media—all in the name of Christianity! And sadly to say, many Christians went right along believing these false accusations!

Is it any wonder, then, why there is so much division in the Church? Division's number one objective is to create strife within the body of Christ which in turn triggers all of the other aspects of warfare. There is a spiritual world-war going on inside the Church today because satan knows that his time to deceive the world is drawing to an end, and his final point of attack is to cause division within the people of God.

It is evident that not all of the troops in God's army are in agreement and walking in unity. This is how it was for the troops that Deborah and Barak had to contend with when they were sent out to deploy men for their varied assignments to fight against Sisera and his army as recorded in Judges 5:15-17:

> **And the princes of Issachar were with Deborah; as Issachar, so was Barak sent into the valley under his command; AMONG THE DIVISIONS OF REUBEN THERE WERE GREAT RESOLVES OF HEART (emphasis mine);**
>
> **Verse 15**
>
> **Why did you sit among the sheepfolds, to hear the pipings for the flocks? The divisions of Reuben have great searchings of heart.**
>
> **Verse 16**

And,

> **Gilead stayed beyond the Jordon, and why did Dan remain on ships? Asher continued at the seashore, and stayed by his inlets.**
>
> **Verse 17**

In this special mission, God sent alongside Deborah and Barak **men who had understanding of the times** (1 Chronicles 12:32), the princes of Issachar. These prophets not only understood the battle plan laid out before their mission, but they also understood the deceptive strategies the spirit of division had caused within God's troops. It was Barak's assignment, along with Deborah and the other prophets, to go down to the valley of

Reuben to deploy the troops there for their assigned position of duty.

Former U.S. military commander, Norman Schwarzkopf, once said,

> *"Whether we're talking about a spiritual battle or one here on earth, you always have to look at the mission, the enemy, the terrain, and the troops available. You generally know three things if you've done your homework: You know the mission, you know the terrain, and you know the reserves available."*

We know that the enemy has come to steal, kill and destroy the vision of the Church. Unfortunately for this troop, Deborah and Barak found **"great divisions among Reueben."** Everyone had found their own comfortable position, their own devised theology, and their varies excuses and blockades for not going to the front line of battle.

THIS LAND IS YOUR LAND, THIS LAND IS MY LAND

After entering the Promised Land, the tribes of Israel had been scattered throughout the regions of Canaan. Nobody knows the exact boundaries of the Promised Land, however, God revealed to Abraham the land he and his descendants would receive—**from the river of Egypt to the River Euphrates** (Genesis 15:18). And, God originally promised them a larger area than they received.

Several hundred years later, when Moses reminded the Israelites of that promise, he revealed to them the boundaries of the Promised Land in Deuteronomy 1:7: **The Arabah** (the mountain regions), **the Shephelah, and the Negev and the coastal plains by the Mediteranean Sea, from the southern border of Canaan through Lebanon up to the Euphrates.** In short, that's-a-lotta-territory!

By this time, the Israelites already lived in the Transjordan (the land east and south of the Jordan River), and God allowed the tribes of Reuben and Gad, as well as part of the tribe of Manasseh, to settle in the newly occupied land of the Amorites which is east of the Jordan river (see Numbers 21:21 and 35:32).

However, during the conquest of Canaan, the people of Israel **failed to take the total area promised to them**, partly because they were unfaithful to God through their "complacency." God punished the Israelites by holding them back from complete victory:

For forty years I was grieved with that generation and said, "It is a people who go astray in their hearts, and do not know My ways." So I swore in My wrath, "They shall not enter My rest."

Psalm 95:10-11

Some of the tribes of Israel lacked part of their inheritance because of their own affections. When they came to the Promised Land their hearts were set on finding endless valleys of crops and hillsides adorned with grasses, herbs and flowers. But because of their disobedience and lack of faith, they instead found thorns and thistles. What the Israelites could accomplish from the soil of Palestine **would depend entirely upon their relationship with the Lord.** God promised to bless them for their obedience:

The Lord will open to you His good treasure, the heavens, to give the rain to your land in its season, and to bless all the work of your hand...

Deuteronomy 28:12

Disobedience, however, blocked all of the blessings God had intended to pour out upon His people. The tribes of Reuben and Gad and part of the tribe of Manasseh eventually received their inheritance east of the Jordan River, as they had requested. However, the prospect of still be separated from the other tribes troubled them, and **eventually caused great divisions among all the tribes.**

For the Christian, the crossing over into our Promised Land was made simple and easy at Calvary through the precious atoning blood of Jesus Christ. Because of our unrighteousness, **God made Him who knew no sin to be sin for us, that we might become the righteousness of God in Him** (2 Corinthians 5:21). When we crossed over from our sinful bounding death into our promised victorious life in Jesus Christ, those same promises that God made to Abraham and his descendants became our inheritance. God's promise in Genesis 22:17-18 is the same promise for you and I today!

> **In blessing I will bless thee, and in multiplying I will multiply thy seed as the stars of the heaven, and as the sand which is upon the sea shore; and thy seed shall possess the gate of his enemies! And in thy seed shall all nations of the earth be blessed; because thou hast obeyed My voice (KJV).**

Why, then, since we are one Body through the promised possession of heavenly treasures, is there still great division in the body of Christ today? There were many different excuses created by the troops of Deborah's time that caused blockades that restricted God's people from entering into their assigned positions. These very same excuses and blockades still exist today in the Church.

BLOCKADE #1: DIVISION & ENTERTAINMENT

> **Among the divisions of Reuben there were great resolves of heart. Why did you sit among the sheepfolds, to hear the pipings of the flocks? The divisions of Reuben have great searchings of heart.**
>
> **Judges 5:15b-16**

Reuben. Declining from service, Reuben had long ago been deprived of the privileges of the birthright (Genesis 49:3-4) and declared by his father, Jacob, **unstable as water, he shall not excel.** Because of these downfalls, Reuben took two steps backwards from the call of God by their division and self-centered affections.

Nothing could please our heavenly Father more than for Him to see His children walking in unity (Psalm 133). But Reuben couldn't come into agreement with the rest of God's people. Even though they had some petty disagreements, it shouldn't have hindered them from following God's orders to report to duty for a great cause. Instead of uniting together under the will of God, they became bordered through strife and self-centeredness. They thought they had the right formula above all the others to succeed in their land of promise.

Another blockade Reuben had erected was a self-centered affection towards a lifestyle of leisure. Reuben **dwelt among the sheepfolds,** a comfortable, simplified and safer place than the front line of battle. They loved to hear the **pipings for the flocks,** an entertaining sound made through flutes, oaten reeds or pipes. Thus, the people were conditioned to a comfortable, entertaining and peaceable style of living. They were too fearful of the thought of going to battle, and because they stubbornly refused to let go of the comforts and security of their peaceful valley, Reuben stayed with the sheepfolds. Reuben was a people who were divided and self-centered toward their own affections.

BLOCKADE #2: LACK OF VISION

Gilead stayed beyond the Jordan…

Judges 5:17a

Gilead. Ten cities from the regions of southern Bashan and northern Gilead organized to form the Decapolis, the "politically-correct" politicians Jesus mentions in Matthew 4:25 and

Mark 5:20. Each city was a strategic point in the political divisions of the region. The mountains of Gilead lay east of the region in Samaria with an abundance of vegetation and evergreens. The sap extracted from these evergreens were used for medicinal purposes, which is known as the famous "healing balm of Gilead."

Half of the tribe of Manasseh settled in these mountains which were covered with thick, dense brushwood and oaks. You might say that the people of Gilead *couldn't see the forest for the trees* because of the mountain's dense forestry.

During my childhood, I remember our usual family drive up to Mount Rainier from our home in Tacoma, Washington. We could see the mountain peak from our very backyard, and as we drove closer towards the mountainside, the trees got larger and greener. As we reached the winding roads alongside of the mountain, rows of towering pine trees began to enclose us within the two-lane highway, and the sky almost disappeared from our view. Hiking into the deep wooded areas, the only visible signs of life were the towering pines and brushwood. We lost all sight of the city life and all of its smell as well! Mount Rainier was our "get-away-from-it-all" retreat, and literally speaking, we lost sight of all other things.

This is what happened to the people of Gilead. They became so accustomed to the dense forestry, they lost sight of the vision that God had given them in order to move them from their mountain into their positioned they were appointed.

Gilead was also a place of refuge as well. When Elijah faced a three-year famine, he stayed by the Brook of Cherith in Gilead where the water refreshed him and the ravens brought him food (1 Kings 17:3). Even so, the people of Gilead declined their appointed position of duty because they became accustomed to the safety and serenity of this glorious refuge.

In similarity, the body of Christ has become accustomed to the safety and serenity of "thrill-me" hours of church services, rather than a well-balanced diet of praise and worship, evangelism, teaching and fellowship. The forestry inside the sanctuary has become so dense for some Christians, that many can't see beyond the trees to get outside the church door. When Elijah had received his strength and balance, God moved him out on his way again. Gilead was a people who lost sight of the vision that God had given them.

BLOCKADE #3: IDOLATRY

And why did Dan remain on ships?
Judges 5:17a

Dan. God originally had given the coastal plains to the tribe of Dan for their inheritance. However, later on, the Philistines overpowered them and caused the Danites to relocate in the upper Jordan Valley (Judges 18:27-31). But, during the time of Deborah, Dan was located on the coastal plains where ships flowed to the Sea of Galilee and the Dead Sea via the Jordan River.

This region has been the center of Israel's social and economical life, both in ancient times and today. The vast economic system was centered in this city governed by the people of Dan. From history, many of its residents were wealthy and rich by the abundance of the world's sea trading. Even gorillas were a high-profit trade item transported by the ships of Dan! For most of their lives, the people of Dan were accustomed to the luxurious and secure living conditions by an abundance of economical wealth. When God called Dan to the appointed position of duty, the people declined service because of their idolatry of mammon, the love of money above the call of God. Dan was a people who sought to serve both God and materialism.

BLOCKADE #4: BUSYNESS

Asher continued at the seashore, and stayed by his inlets.

Judges 5:17b

Asher. The small plain of Asher extends five miles wide between Phoenicia and Egypt, stretching along the coast of the Great Sea. Because of its strategic location, Asher was an important center for commerce. Because of its importance for commercial trading, the people of Asher were a "busy" people with extensive business for the region to meet the world's trading market. They were the wallstreet of their times. Because of their wealth and time-consuming laboring, the people of Asher were "too busy" to respond to the call of duty when God sent for them. The priorities of "busyness" became their blockade to continue by the seashore. Asher was a people too busy for God's work.

There are various excuses that have erected blockades in the Church today which have restricted God's people from responding to the call of duty. Division, Self-Centeredness, Entertainment, Lack of Vision, Idolatry, and Busyness.

Division continues to remain the number one stronghold within the body of Christ today. It has hindered many divine strategies to benefit the kingdom of God and has kept many Christians from living victorious lives. Many have been called and have fully committed their heart, mind and soul to the call of God, yet they have allowed a spirit of division to hinder them from fulfilling a great mission. Without compromising Biblical truths, we must walk in unity, **for how can two walk together unless they are agreed?** (Amos 3:3). We must let the walls of petty disagreements fall down and allow God's grace to reign in each of us. If the body of Christ fails to repent, disarm and denounce the spirit of division in the Church, then this final hour for end-time ministry will greatly suffer.

However, God says that His Word, His plan, His vision, **shall not return to Him void.** He will position those who respond to the call of duty. The next chapter will reveal those who were faithful and **jeopardized their lives** for the sake of God's call.

CHAPTER FOUR

A CALL TO DUTY

My heart is with the rulers of Israel who offered themselves willingly with the people...

Judges 5:9

As the body of Christ continues to be drawn closer together in this hour, God is seeking those who are willing to submit and offer themselves without reservation to Him and His people in order to take on the divine strategies He has laid out for the fulfillment of His kingdom.

In order to do this, the church must be loosed from all earthly matters, and bound to heavenly realities. By faith, Christians must know and trust God's Word, His will, His voice and His Holy Spirit to lead and guide their every move. And regardless of the offenses we may incur, we must love one another unconditionally.

God is calling such a people to appointed positions in the body of Christ for a great end-time move of His Holy Spirit. Miracle signs and wonders will release the kingdom of God upon the entire world before Jesus returns, causing many to repent and be saved.

I believe 100% of the harvest is ready, but I believe 80% of the church in the western world is NOT ready. As I mentioned earlier, I believe the body of Christ will greatly suffer if we fail to repent of our disobedience from not responding to the call of duty in this final hour.

However, God will not allow His kingdom to go unfinished. He may be denied by His own, yet He will not deny His Word, His plan, and His vision---it SHALL be fulfilled.

In the time of Deborah, God had appointed certain faithful men and women of God from various backgrounds to fulfill a great mission. Though many of the other tribes failed to respond to their call to duty, these faithful tribes fully submitted to the call and came to the frontline of battle by faith and obedience. Even though each tribe was unique and different in its origin and purpose, each tribe responded in unity and submitted to the will of God.

ZEBULUN AND NAPHTALI

Zebulun is a people who jeopardized their lives to the point of death...Naphtali also on the heights of the battlefield.

Judges 5:18

Zebulun (Zeb-oo-loon) and Naphtali (Nof-tal-lee) are known historically and today as the place of a great light. Jesus dwelt in Capernaum which was bordered by Zebulun and Naphtali by the Sea of Galilee. As prophesied by Isaiah, Zebulun and Naphtali was a strategic location where a great light would dwell:

> **The people who walked in darkness have seen a great light; those who dwelt in the land of the shadow of death, upon them a light has shined.**
>
> **Isaiah 9:2**

Zebulun and Naphtali was the location where Jesus began His earthly ministry and many people were saved, delivered and healed (Matthew 4:12-17). It was a remote part of the country, set apart from the rest of the world, and was a safe haven for incoming ships.

Zebulun and Naphtali was a "sanctuary" of the region, set apart by the Holy Spirit of God. It was the place where Jesus was welcomed, where elsewhere He had been rejected.

In the time of Deborah, Zebulun was a faithful tribe who "jeopardized their lives to the point of death," and responded to the call of God without hesitation. They had been set apart for a certain time and task which demanded holiness and sanctification. They were a place of great light; the lighthouse for other incoming tribes to seek their commanding orders. Like the beginning of Jesus' earthly ministry, Zebulun was a people sent out to preach the kingdom of God.

Naphtali likewise was faithful to respond to the call of God. By the origin of their name (Naphtaliy), they were a people who "wrestled" among the people, causing division and strife. However, through their obedience to God, they dwelt in unity because they had made God their sanctuary of peace.

Their position was stationed "*on the heights of the battlefield,*" a place only where "watchmen" could be positioned. These people were the voice of God who gave the commanding orders to the various troops. It was also a risk of their own lives, and to the point of death. Yet, Naphtali sought only the will of God for that hour.

EPHRAIM

Out of Ephraim was there a root of them against Amalek...

Judges 5:14, KJV

Ephraim, which is located on the western region of Canaan, was not anywhere near the battlefield. In fact, the people of Ephraim were dwelling in the mountain regions occupied by the

Amalekites. Joshua fought against Amalek with great zeal and boldness in his days. The tribe of Ephraim also had plenty of experience in warfare with the Amalekites, which had produced a great zeal and boldness within them.

The people of Ephraim, meaning "*fruitfulness*" had also been equipped with the fruit of the Spirit in order to be positioned in the enemies' territory: Love, joy, peace, long-suffering, kindness, goodness, faithfulness, gentleness, and self-control. They were fruitful in the land they had so faithfully sown into. God appointed Ephraim to their position of duty because they had exhibited zeal, boldness, and all of the fruit of the Spirit.

BENJAMIN

After you Benjamin with your peoples.
Judges 5:14a

Benjamin, as well as Ephraim, also dwelt among the Amalekites. Though their tribe was much smaller than those of Ephraim, they were still equally important and equally strong for the position of their calling.

Benjamin, meaning "*right arm,*" was positioned to be a great pillar and support to the army of God. When Moses sent out Joshua and the army of the Lord against Amalek (Exodus 17:8-16), Aaron and Hur supported Moses' hands by holding them up until victory had been won.

God is appointing to position a people like Benjamin who will position themselves as servants within the kingdom of God, always willing to encourage and lift up the faint-hearted. These are the canteen men---the water bearers who refresh God's wearied army.

MACHIR

...From Machir rulers came down...

Judges 5:14b

The people of Machir were descendants of the tribe of Manasseh who dwelt southeast of the Jabbok River (Joshua 13:31). In the story of 2 Samuel 17, David escapes to the region of Mahanaim, a city just east of the Jordan River and occupied by the people of Machir.

When David reached Mahanaim, the people of Machir, along with several other tribes, brought supplies to David and his army such as, "*beds and basins, earthen vessels and wheat, barley and flour, parched grain and beans, lentils and parched seeds, honey and curds, sheep and cheese of the herd, for David and the people who were with him to eat*" (vs. 27-29).

In the time of Deborah, the people of Machir were appointed by God to supply the needs of the troops with their provisions of food, clothing and shelter. They were specifically positioned inside the army camp to supply the physical needs of men and women on the battlefield.

Today, God is appointing faithful stewards and cheerful givers in positions to meet the physical needs of the body of Christ. The people of Machir, meaning "*tumble*" and "*perish*" were also once a broken, fallen people whom God restored and prospered for this great service.

THOSE WHO ENLIST

There are many unknown people, yet not unknown to God, who have laid down their lives for the sake of the call. God is seeking and appointing in this final hour those who are faithful, bold, zealous, set apart and unified in His Spirit, humble and fruitful in all things, the least and the smallest, who carry a servant's heart, and are good stewards. His heart is with those who "*willingly offer themselves with the people*" and count all things loss for the gain of His Son, Jesus Christ.

The qualifications for God's service are made simple through obedience, and are mandatory for enlistment into the Lord's army!

CHAPTER FIVE

A.W.O.L.

"Curse Meroz," said the angel of the Lord, "Curse its inhabitants bitterly, because they did not come to the help of the Lord, to the help of the Lord against the mighty."

Judges 5:23

Sometimes being at the wrong place at the wrong time can reap great losses in the kingdom of God. One such tribe in the time of Deborah found this to be true. Meroz, one of the troops enlisted to fight in the battle of Sisera, had been positioned right in the center of frontline duty. According to historical and geographical references, Meroz was the central battle zone of this mission. No one could have been positioned any closer than those of Meroz.

Unlike the other troops who declined their call to duty, Meroz responded by their attendance alone, excluding their qualifications for service. They were present for the roll call, but absent from the action of duty.

UNKNOWN SOLDIERS

I remember one young soldier and friend of mine who served in the Vietnam war. He repeatedly ran away from the army base he was stationed at, only to return and receive repeated A.W.O.L. (Absent Without Leave) pink slips. Over a period of two years, however, the military records got mixed up and his absences began to show up "present" on the personnel attendance records. The army personnel did not recognize his absence for two whole years. But one day, his rebellion caught up with him. After the army personnel found out he had been absent without leave (A.W.O.L.) for 822 days, they immediately discharged him from military duty by a "dishonorable discharge" (DD).

According to the Department of Defense, a "DD" is recorded on the serviceman's personal records for life! All government benefits such as social security, federal tax refunds and exemption benefits, disability or government grants are cancelled and denied to the discharged serviceman. According to the U.S. government, the discharged serviceman is considered "dead" or "unknown" to all federal and state authorities, and society as well.

This is what happened to the people of Meroz. They were absent from the line of duty, though they were positioned for service. They walked away from the active duty they had been called, equipped, and even prepared for. When the trumpet sounded, they were idle and "*did not come to the help of the Lord.*"

Then the angel of the Lord brought them their final pink slip...their "DD": "*Curse Meroz bitterly,*" the angel of the Lord announced. God does not take AWOL's lightly---He means serious business in the kingdom of God! Meroz lost all of the blessings of God; all of the abundance of joy, peace and fruitfulness was dismissed from their lives. And, according to Biblical reference, the name *Meroz* is undefined, without any meaning, and is never again mentioned in the Bible. They had no honor to keep their namesake, or to ever again claim their territorial inheritance.

THE GREATEST HEROES OF ALL

In the army of the Lord, the consequences of disobedience are not too far from the same, EXCEPT that in His kingdom we now serve a God of grace. Where dishonorable discharges were issued, He also provides those who repent with an "honorable re-charge" to position us back into His perfect will.

In the world's army, the greatest American heroes are given an honorable "purple heart" medallion for their outstanding heroic actions in the line of duty. But in the Lord's army, those who **repent and return to Him are the greatest heroes of all!** "*Return to the Lord,*" He says, "*And He will return to you*" (Zechariah 1:3).

By God's abounding grace, those who have strayed from the call to duty can return to the Father's open arms and be the hero of His eye. All of the pink slips are destroyed and forgotten, and in place, we are given a purified clean heart.

BATTLE CRY

As in the time of Deborah, the body of Christ today is crying out for a fresh Word from God so that His perfect will can be done through us on this earth. There are many Christians who hunger and thirst for a fresh anointing of God so that they may become vessels who will contain the true glory of God. Those who are drawing near to the front line of battle are crying out, "*Abba, Father, all things are possible for You. Take this cup away from me; nevertheless, NOT what I WILL, but what YOU WILL*" (Mark 14:36).

I believe the Lord would answer our cry with these words:

"Write the vision and make it plain on the tablets that he may run who reads it. For the vision is yet for an APPOINTED TIME, but at the end it will SPEAK, and it will not lie. Though it tarries, WAIT FOR IT; because it WILL SURELY COME, it will not tarry."

Habakkuk 2:2-3

Has God placed a vision in your heart? Do you desire to become a vessel who will contain the true glory of the Lord? Do you believe all things are possible for God to bring your vision to pass? If so, then only trust His Word, for "*though it tarries...wait for it...it will surely come.*" Be equipped AND prepared! ***"...Position yourselves, stand still and see the salvation of the Lord, who is with you..."*** (2 Chronicles 20:17).

SELECTED BIBLIOGRAPHY

Chapter One

[1]McIntosh, Gary, *The Father's Discipline,* Riverside, California; Logos to Rhema Publishers, 1991.

[2]Hamon, Dr. Bill, *Prophets, Pitfalls and Principles,* Shippensburg, Pennsylvania; Destiny Image Publishers, 1991.

Other Suggested Reading

Clement, Kim, *The Sound of His Voice,* Lake Mary, Florida; Creation House, 1993.

Hagin, Kenneth E., *How You Can Be Led By The Spirit of God,* Tulsa, Oklahoma; Faith Library Publications, 1978.

Hagin, Kenneth E., *The Gift of Prophecy,* Tulsa, Oklahoma; Faith Library Publications, 1985.

ABOUT THE AUTHOR

Linda Montgomery founded *Passion for Purpose Ministries* as a ministry of encouragement and spiritual empowerment to the body of Christ through Bible teaching and ministry. Since 1987, she has developed new ministries, assisted in church planting, trained leaders, founded and helped lead city-wide prayer gatherings for pastors and leaders, coordinated and led conferences, led praise and worship, as well as preaching and teaching in various churches. She has also appeared on Christian radio and television programs discussing various Bible topics and ministering in prayer.

The vision for *Passion for Purpose Ministries* is to develop, launch and nurture creative ministries to bring the very simple, non-religious message of Jesus Christ to the people of Los Angeles, Hollywood and Orange County, networking with the creative arts, media and local churches. This mission also extends to the entire world that they may know and experience Jesus Christ. Linda Montgomery's compassion and desire to develop and launch new leaders into their God-ordained purpose challenges all believers in their faith, unity of the body of Christ, and obedience to the end-time call of God.

In the early years of her ministry, Linda Montgomery founded, *Spirit of Truth Ministries,* where she functions primarily in the prophetic ministry to the body of Christ, as well as evangelism to cults, specifically the New Age religion. As a result, her teaching expanded into the prophetic ministry for healing, deliverance and restoration.

Linda Montgomery is also an author, writer and publisher with a variety of published works including, *A Call To Duty---God's Call for Spiritual Positioning in the Body of Christ for End-Time Ministry; The Devil Didn't Make Me Do It!---A Simple Guide to Understanding Spiritual Warfare;* and, *The Discovery of Leadership: Discovering God's Purpose and Principles for Effective Leadership.* She has also authored many other articles and periodicals for Christian organizations.

For more information send email to:

Contact Email: **om**

PassionForPurpose2000@gmail.com